**This edition first published in 2008
by Franklin Watts**

Franklin Watts
338 Euston Road
London NW1 3BH

Franklin Watts Australia
Level 17/207 Kent Street
Sydney, NSW 2000

© 2008 The Brown Reference Group plc
First Floor, 9-17 St. Albans Place
London N1 ONX

www.brownreference.com

ISBN: 978-0-7496-8414-3

Dewey number: 940.3

Editor: Peter Darman
Children's Publisher: Anne O'Daly
Editorial Director: Lindsey Lowe
Creative Director: Jeni Child
Designer: Reg Cox

Photographic credits:
All photographs the Robert Hunt Library except the following;
Mary Evans Picture Library: 28 (top)

This book is dedicated to the memory of Ernst Junger,
World War I veteran and author of *Storm of Steel*

Printed in the United States

Franklin Watts is a division of Hachette Children's Books,
an Hachette Livre UK company.
www.hachettelivre.co.uk

Introduction

The origins of World War I lay in the late 19th century. The major European powers – Britain, France, Germany and Russia – controlled colonies in Africa and Asia. Colonies provided valuable raw materials, such as oil and cotton, and valuable markets to sell finished goods. The European powers spread their influence so widely that by 1914 they ruled 85 percent of the world.

Colonies needed to be defended. Colonisation went hand-in-hand with a build-up of weapons, as European powers tried to defend their own trade. Everyone had to keep up with the military power of their neighbours. This was known as an arms race. Meanwhile, weapons were becoming more powerful, more deadly and – thanks to mass production – available in huge numbers.

The naval arms race

The arms race also took place at sea. In the late 1890s Britain, which had the most colonies, had the world's largest navy. Its naval strength was challenged by both France and Russia. The British built more warships. Britain's rapid production of ships, however, sparked a naval arms race with Germany. Now the British answer was to build better warships. In 1906 they built the battleship HMS *Dreadnought*. It was far superior to any vessel afloat. It was not long before Britain's rivals began building their own Dreadnought-type battleships.

Europe's powers also tried to maintain the arms balance by entering into a series of

alliances with other countries. Germany became allied with Austria-Hungary and Italy. The members of this Triple Alliance were known as the Central Powers. Against them were Britain, France and Russia: the *Triple Entente* or Allies. An attack on any member of either alliance would be considered an attack on all three.

A reason for war

Kaiser Wilhelm of Germany wanted to conquer parts of Russian-dominated eastern Europe. An unprovoked attack on Russia, however, would also mean war with its ally, France. The Germans would then be fighting in both the east and the west. If Germany was to expand into eastern Europe, therefore, it needed a reason to go to war.

If war came, it was still likely that Germany would face war on two fronts. The Germans

When World War I began, Europe was divided into two sides – the Triple Alliance and the *Triple Entente*.

therefore devised a plan. They would attack and defeat France before Russia had time to march its armies west.

The plan involved an advance through Belgium, whose coalfields would be valuable to Germany's economy. Belgium was a neutral state. It was not part of either alliance – but its neutrality was guaranteed by Britain.

Trouble in the Balkans

The flashpoint between the two alliances came in the Balkans. The area was home to many ethnic groups who wanted to create strong countries. The Serbs, for example, wanted to set up a "Greater Serbia." Such a move would threaten Austria-Hungary, which was protected by Germany. Serbia's security, meanwhile, was defended by Russia.

On 28 June, 1914, the heir to the Austro-Hungarian throne, Archduke Franz Ferdinand, was killed by a Serbian terrorist. It happened in Sarajevo, the capital of Bosnia, which was an Austro-Hungarian province. The Austro-Hungarians declared war on Serbia. Germany, knowing that Russia would help Serbia, declared war on Russia. It also declared war on France and Belgium, hoping to defeat them before taking on Russia. In turn, Britain declared war on Germany – World War I had begun.

Germany's Kaiser Wilhelm (centre, left) at a German Army training exercise before the outbreak of World War I.

EYEWITNESS: Captain A. O. Pollard, British officer in Flanders, 1914

"What a shock met my eyes as I mounted the German parapet. The trench was full of men; men with sightless eyes and waxen faces. Each gripped his rifle and leaned against the side of the trench in an attitude of defence, but all were dead. We were attacking a position held by corpses! For a single moment I could not believe my eyes. I though it must be some trick of the Germans to fill the trench with dummies."

28 JUNE, 1914, Bosnia

Archduke Franz Ferdinand, heir to the throne of the Austro-Hungarian Empire, and his wife are killed by a Serbian terrorist in Sarajevo, the capital of Bosnia. Bosnia is a part of the empire. Austria-Hungary suspects the Serb government of being involved in the plot.

25 JULY Serbia

Serbia rejects Austro-Hungarian demands that Serbia becomes part of their empire. The Austrian emperor Franz Joseph orders his army to prepare for war with the Serbians. Russia's emperor, Czar Nicholas II, orders his troops to prepare to protect Serbia from any Austro-Hungarian invasion.

1 AUGUST Germany

Germany, an ally of Austria-Hungary, declares war on Russia at 19:10 hours.

3 AUGUST Germany

Germany declares war on France, which is an ally of Russia. Italy declares itself neutral, meaning that it will stay out of any fighting. This angers its partners in the Triple Alliance – Germany and Austria-Hungary. The Italians argue that Austria-Hungary's attack on Serbia is an act of war. It is therefore not covered by the defensive terms of the Triple Alliance.

4 AUGUST Britain

Germany rejects Britain's demand that its troops leave Belgian soil. The British declare war on Germany at 23:00 hours.

4 AUGUST United States

The U.S. government declares iself neutral.

5 AUGUST Belgium

German troops attack Liège but fail to capture any of the 12 powerful forts protecting the city. Liège is the key border defence in eastern Belgium and a railway centre. It also blocks the

Archduke Franz Ferdinand (centre) and his wife (left) before they were shot.

Neutral – not taking sides in a dispute or war.

planned advance of German forces to the French border, where they plan to swing south towards Paris.

French troops with a guard dog keep watch for German troops, August 1914.

7 AUGUST France

The first members of the 100,000-strong British Expeditionary Force reach France.

8 AUGUST Britain

Field Marshal Sir Horatio Herbert Kitchener, the recently appointed secretary of war, calls for 100,000 volunteers to join the British army. He later poses for a famous recruitment poster. The poster shows Kitchener pointing an accusing finger at the viewer and stating 'Your Country Needs You'.

10 AUGUST Belgium

The first of Liège's 12 forts falls to the Germans following a pounding by large howitzer guns.

12 AUGUST Serbia

Some 200,000 Austro-Hungarian troops invade Serbia. Although they are outnumbered, Serbian forces put up strong resistance in the Battle of the Jadar River. They force the invaders to begin withdrawing on 16 August; five days later, the invasion has been defeated.

TURNING POINTS: The Schlieffen Plan

Germany lay between two potential enemies, France and Russia. The German military planner Alfred von Schlieffen designed a plan to prevent Germany fighting a major war on two fronts. Most of the German Army would attack through Belgium and Holland and then on to Paris. A small part of the army would hold the Russians in the east until German forces, fresh from their rapid victory over France, could be rushed east to defeat Russia. The plan depended on the fast movement of troops by rail.

Key:
→ German attacks
➡ Anglo-French attacks
▬ Anglo-French armies
▬ German armies
— Front, 5 September
▪▪ Front, 14 September
-- Borders

0 — 30 miles
0 — 48 km

Howitzer – a type of field gun.

KEY UNITS: The British Expeditionary Force

At the start of World War I, Britain's army was an all-volunteer force. Its infantry regiments (at right) were highly trained and famous for the volume and accuracy of their rifle fire. The army Britain sent to France in 1914 was called the British Expeditionary Force. It consisted of around 100,000 men. It was well armed, but was later found to be lacking heavy, trench-busting artillery. It was also short of machine guns – just 120 in August 1914. The German Army, by comparison, had 10,500 machine guns.

14 AUGUST France

Two French armies attack German forces near Metz. This is the first of a series of clashes known as the 'Battle of the Frontiers'. A German counter-attack on 20 August forces the French back, however.

16 AUGUST Belgium

After days of German shelling, Liège surrenders. This allows the German First and Second Armies to push west towards France.

A German 42-cm (17-in) howitzer is readied for action in France.

17 AUGUST East Prussia

German troops defeat Russian invaders at Stallupönen. The Russians suffer 3,000 casualties and retreat. The two Russian armies in East Prussia are now separated by a region of swamps and lakes and are short of weapons.

18 AUGUST Belgium

King Albert orders the Belgian Army – 75,000 men – to retreat to the port of Antwerp, which has a garrison of 60,000 men.

19 AUGUST Belgium

German troops shoot 150 civilians at Aerschot. The killing is part of a war policy known as *Shrecklichkeit* ('frightfulness'). It aims to terrify civilians in occupied areas so that they are too afraid to rebel.

20–25 AUGUST Belgium

The 'Battle of the Frontiers' switches to the wooded Ardennes region north of Metz. Two

Counter-attack – an attack by a defending force.

advancing French armies run into two German armies. Three days of confused fighting follow. The French Third Army is almost destroyed before the French fall back to positions between the Meuse and Marne rivers.

22–23 AUGUST Belgium

The third clash of the 'Battle of the Frontiers'. The French Fifth Army fights between the Sambre and Meuse rivers to block the German attack into France. The French retreat after heavy losses. Meanwhile, German artillery is pounding the Belgian fortress of Namur. It falls on 25 August.

23 AUGUST Belgium

At Mons, in another clash of the 'Battle of the Frontiers', the British Expeditionary Force fights the German First Army. Although

Some of the 90,000 Russian prisoners captured at the Battle of Tannenberg.

heavily outnumbered, the British drive back the first German attack. The British then retreat. Mons marks the end of the 'Battle of the Frontiers'. The French have lost 300,000 men.

24 AUGUST East Prussia

German troops delay the Russian advance in East Prussia at the Battle of Orlau-Frankenau. This gives other German units time to gather at nearby Tannenberg. The Russians do not know that their radio messages are being intercepted. The Germans know the enemy's plans.

25–27 AUGUST France

The British Expeditionary Force continues to retreat south, fighting off attacks. At Le Cateau, the British II Corps (40,000 men) fights for its survival as the Germans try to surround it. The British beat off the German attacks, but lose 7,800 men.

26 AUGUST East Prussia

The Germans attack the Russian Second Army at Tannenberg from the north and south, and in the centre. By nightfall on 29 August the Russians are surrounded. Their huge final losses include 90,000 men captured. The defeat ends the Russian invasion of East Prussia.

EYEWITNESS: General von Hindenburg, August 1914

"The ring round thousands and thousands of Russians began to close. Even in this desperate situation there was plenty of Russian heroism in the cause of the Czar, heroism which saved the honour of arms but could no longer save the battle. The lust for battle in our men quickly ebbed away and changed to deep sympathy and human feeling."

Expeditionary force – part of an army sent to fight in a foreign country.

British troops under German artillery fire during the Battle of the Marne.

30 AUGUST France

Paris becomes the first capital city to suffer air attack when a German aeroplane drops four small bombs and propaganda leaflets.

3 SEPTEMBER Galicia

An Austro-Hungarian offensive into Poland meets with disaster. The Russian Fifth Army splits two Austro-Hungarian armies at the Battle of Rava Ruska. This forces the Austro-Hungarians to retreat 160 km (100 miles). By 11 September, the Austro-Hungarians lose 350,000 men – killed, wounded or taken prisoner.

28 AUGUST North Sea

British warships meet the German High Seas Fleet in German waters. The clash, known as the Battle of Heligoland Bight, begins at 07:00 hours. British warships catch the Germans by surprise. However, the Germans recover and their more powerful vessels advance to attack. British reinforcements then arrive to cover the withdrawal of the first British force. The British lose no ships, but they send four German vessels to the bottom.

5 SEPTEMBER France

The Battle of the Marne. French and British forces counterattack along the Marne River between Paris and Verdun.

5–9 SEPTEMBER France

The Battle of the Ourcq. As part of the Marne Offensive, the French Sixth Army attacks the right flank of the German First Army east of

KEY PEOPLE: Snipers

Snipers (right) were highly skilled marksmen who shot enemy troops with a rifle. The presence of a sniper at the front forced the enemy to take more care and helped to undermine morale, because a sniper was difficult to spot. Trench warfare allowed snipers to get close to the enemy. Some even crawled into No-Man's Land between the lines of trenches in the dark. Many snipers had a spotter with binoculars to identify targets. A sniper would sometimes wait for hours before he took a shot.

Propaganda – material that spreads ideas or rumours to help one side in a war.

Paris. German counter-attacks come close to breaking the French line. Only reinforcements arriving from Paris in a fleet of taxicabs prevent a French defeat.

Belgian troops destroy a rail bridge to slow the advance of the German Army.

7 SEPTEMBER Serbia

The Battle of the Drina River. Austro-Hungarian troops launch a second invasion of Serbia. After 10 days of intense combat, the Serbs retreat to Belgrade, the Serbian capital.

9 SEPTEMBER France

The German First and Second Armies withdraw from their positions near Paris. This ends the Battle of the Marne. The Germans have suffered a decisive defeat. The original Schlieffen Plan called for a sweeping victory over France in the first few weeks of the war. The Battle of the Marne makes this impossible. Germany now faces a war on two fronts.

9 SEPTEMBER East Prussia

The Germans attempt to surround the Russian First Army at the Masurian Lakes. Although many Russian soldiers escape, the operation is a major German success. The Russians lose 125,000 men killed, wounded or captured. German casualties total 40,000.

15–18 SEPTEMBER France

The Battle of the Aisne. The British and French attack the withdrawing Germans, but with little success. Both sides now attempt to outflank each other – the Germans by attacking the French and British left flank, the French and British in turn striking against the German right flank. A number of similar actions gradually take the rival forces closer to the North Sea coast. The series of manoeuvres becomes known as the 'Race to the Sea'.

22 SEPTEMBER North Sea

The German submarine *U-9* sinks the British cruisers *Aboukir*, *Hogue* and *Cressy* off the Dutch coast. More than 1,400 men die.

EYEWITNESS: Captain Louis Madelin, French Army, 1914

"I have with the colours three brothers, two brothers-in-law, three nephews, eighteen to nineteen years old, and these men are soldiers of all grades in every rank of the army. They write letters fairly brimming with courage. Some of them have been wounded, but they returned as soon as possible to the firing line. One of my brothers took some Alsatian villages. He saw the colonel of his battalion of Chasseurs (cavalry) fall."

Flank – the right or left wing of an army.

TURNING POINTS: The Christmas Truce

By Christmas 1914 the soldiers on the Western Front were exhausted. At dawn on Christmas Day, the British in trenches near the Belgian city of Ypres heard carols coming from German positions. They then saw Christmas trees being placed along the trenches. German soldiers climbed out of their trenches into No-Man's Land and called on the British to join them. The two sides met (at right) between the trenches, exchanged gifts, talked and played football. Then they went back to war.

16 OCTOBER New Zealand

The New Zealand Expeditionary Force sails from Wellington to fight for the British in France.

17 OCTOBER Australia

Around 20,000 Australian troops set out to fight with the British on the Western Front.

18–28 OCTOBER France/Belgium

The Germans try but fail to capture the Channel ports used by the British. To the north, Belgian forces struggle to stop the Germans. Eventually, King Albert orders the opening of canal and sea-defence sluice gates. This floods a key area in the path of the German advance. On 19 October, the British counter-attack the Germans around the Belgian city of Ypres. They become bogged down in low-lying fields turned to thick mud by heavy rains.

29 OCTOBER Turkey

The Turkish government declares war on Russia. The Turkish fleet bombards the Russian ports of Odessa, Sevastopol and Theodosia. Turkey's siding with the Central Powers closes the Dardanelles, the vital seaway linking the Mediterranean to the Black Sea. This stops France and Britain sending supplies to Russia.

29 OCTOBER–24 NOVEMBER Belgium

The First Battle of Ypres. The German Fourth and Sixth Armies try to break through to the Channel ports of Calais and Boulogne.

Serbian troops attack the Austro-Hungarians near Belgrade.

Bombard – to attack with artillery.

The *Gneisenau*, the German cruiser sunk at the Battle of the Falklands.

8 DECEMBER South Atlantic Ocean

Five German warships are surprised by a British squadron at the Battle of the Falklands, off Argentina. The British sink two armoured cruisers: the *Scharnhorst*, the German flagship, and the *Gneisenau*. The light cruisers *Nürnberg* and *Leipzig* are also sent to the bottom. Only one German ship escapes from the battle, the light cruiser *Dresden*.

14 DECEMBER France/Belgium

The French and British launch an offensive along the Western Front, from the North Sea to Verdun. Poor weather and strong German defences mean that they make little progress. Only in Champagne, where the French make small gains in return for huge casualties, does fighting go on through the winter. The First Battle of Champagne continues into 1915.

Desperate fighting by the French and British stems the tide. In early November the Germans try again to break through, but fail. Both sides now begin digging trenches, which will soon stretch from the North Sea to the Swiss border.

3 NOVEMBER North Sea

German warships begin to bombard towns along Britain's east coast and to lay mines offshore. The raids reach their peak on 16 December, when German heavy cruisers attack the ports of Whitby and Hartlepool and cause over 700 casualties.

5–30 NOVEMBER Serbia

Facing a renewed Austro-Hungarian attack towards Belgrade and desperately short of ammunition, Serbian troops withdraw. Austro-Hungarian troops occupy the Serbian capital on 2 December.

3–9 DECEMBER Serbia

The Battle of Kolubra. Serbian forces under Marshal Radomir Putnik, now supplied with ammunition by France, smash the invading forces. The Austro-Hungarians lose 230,000 men. Serbian casualties are 170,000 men out of a total of 400,000.

EYEWITNESS: Fred Coleman, British soldier, 1914

"Showers came and went. The roads were deep with mud. The main bridge over the river being impassable, my only alternative was the aqueduct bridge. The artillery had ploughed through, however, so on I went. Ankle-deep in thick mud, slipping, sliding, skidding slowly forward, I at last came to the point where the guns had made a path up the steep bank."

Cruiser – a fast, heavily armed warship.

EYEWITNESS: E. Alexander Powell, U.S. journalist in France, 1915

"There was something strangely oppressive and uncanny about this great stretch of fertile countryside, dotted here and there with white-walled cottages and clumps of farm buildings, but with not a single human being to be seen. On the other side of the opposite ridge I knew that the German batteries were posted, just as the French guns were stationed out of sight at the back of the ridge on which I stood."

13 JANUARY, 1915, Britain

A council of war decides on a naval attack against Turkey. The plan aims to open the Dardanelles channel between the Black Sea and the Mediterranean to the flow of supplies between Russia and France and Britain.

19–20 JANUARY Britain

The Germans launch the first airship raid. Two Zeppelins, the *L3* and *L4*, bomb eastern England. They cause 20 civilian casualties.

24 JANUARY North Sea

In the Battle of the Dogger Bank, ships of the British Home Fleet meet Germany's High Seas Fleet. Admiral Franz von Hipper's German warships are attacked by vessels commanded by Admiral Sir David Beatty. Taken by surprise, Hipper orders a withdrawal. Beatty's faster and better-armed warships sink the *Blücher*, but Hipper's other ships manage to escape.

31 JANUARY Poland

The German Ninth Army under General August von Mackensen attacks towards Warsaw. The Germans begin the advance, known as the Battle of Bolimov, by firing 18,000 poison gas shells at Russian lines. It is the first time poison gas has been used in the war, but the intense cold and winds reduce its impact. Russian counter-attacks on 6 February recapture lost ground but at a cost of 40,000 casualties. German losses total 20,000.

1 FEBRUARY Germany

The government agrees to an unrestricted submarine campaign. This means that German

A German destroyer at the Battle of the Dogger Bank in January 1915.

Zeppelin – a long, thin, motor-powered airship.

vessels can now sink ships of even neutral countries without giving any warning.

7 FEBRUARY East Prussia

The Second Battle of the Masurian Lakes. Field Marshal Paul von Hindenburg begins a double attack against the Russians by sending two armies against the Russian Tenth Army. The German Eighth Army attacks first against the left flank of the Russian Tenth Army. On 8 February, the German Tenth Army attacks the Russians' right flank. By 22 February, the Germans have pushed the Russians back 112 km (70 miles) and taken 90,000 prisoners.

1 MARCH Britain

The government starts a naval-led blockade of Germany to cut off its trade and supplies.

18 MARCH Mediterranean Sea

The final Anglo-French attempt to force a way through the Dardanelles by naval power alone fails. Turkish mines sink three warships from

A German guards Russian prisoners from the Battle of the Masurian Lakes.

the attacking fleet. Three more ships are badly damaged. British Admiral de Robeck orders his surviving warships to withdraw. The British and French decide instead on a land attack aimed at the Turkish capital, Constantinople, via the Gallipoli Peninsula.

KEY WEAPONS: Gas Warfare

Poison gas was first used in the war in 1915. Early gas attacks were launched from cylinders. They needed wind to blow the gas towards the enemy. Later, shells were made comprising a case filled with gas and a small explosive device to crack the casing and allow the gas to escape. Both sides used gas. Mustard gas attacked the body through the lungs, burned the skin and damaged the bloodstream. It could also cause permanent blindness. Gas masks (right) offered protection against gas.

Blockade – the closing off of a country's trade using warships.

A Turkish shell explodes near a British pier at Cape Helles, Gallipoli Peninsula.

a million Armenians have been killed or have died through neglect or starvation.

22 APRIL Belgium

The Second Battle of Ypres begins with the first use of poison chlorine gas on the Western Front. The Germans have 4,000 gas cylinders. Having no protection against the gas, several British units panic and run away. They leave a gap in the frontline some 8 km (5 miles) wide.

5 APRIL France

The French First and Third Armies attack the German-held St. Mihiel salient in the Meuse-Argonne region. Progress is limited due to poor weather, thick mud and the German defences. The attack fizzles out after a few weeks.

8 APRIL Turkey

Turkish troops in Armenia begin a campaign against the independence movement, which has led many Armenians to support the Russians. The Turks kill men and send women and children to other parts of Turkey. By September,

25 APRIL Turkey

The Anglo-French invasion of the Gallipoli Peninsula begins badly. At Cape Helles, a British division comes ashore in the face of heavy Turkish fire. Nevertheless, the British almost reach their chief objectives – the high ground of Achi Baba and the town of Krithia – on 28 April. However, confusion reigns. Some British troops even stop to make tea. The Turks then occupy both positions, from where they can shoot down on the British positions on the beaches below. The Australian and New

KEY PEOPLE: Lord Kitchener

Horatio Herbert Kitchener (1850–1916) was a famous British general before the war. He had fought wars in Sudan in the 1890s and against the Boers in 1899–1902. He was appointed as secretary of war on 3 August, 1914. He realized that World War I was not going to be short and that Britain needed a large army. He eventually succeeded in raising three million volunteers, helped by a famous poster featuring himself (right).

Salient – a part of a frontline that projects into enemy territory.

EYEWITNESS: From the German Embassy, Washington, D.C., 1915

"Travellers intending to embark on the Atlantic Ocean voyage are reminded that a state of war exists between Germany and her allies and Great Britain and her allies; that the zone of war includes the waters adjacent to the British Isles; that vessels flying the flag of Great Britain or any of her allies, are liable to destruction in those waters and that travellers sailing in the war zone do so at their own personal risk."

Zealand Army Corps (ANZAC) meanwhile fails to capture Chunuk Bair Ridge.

26 APRIL Italy

The Italians agree to join the war against their former ally Austria-Hungary. They have been promised Austrian territory in return.

6 MAY Turkey

The British at Gallipoli try to capture the town of Krithia. They fail and lose 6,500 men.

7 MAY Atlantic Ocean

The *Lusitania* is sunk by the German submarine *U-20*. Among the dead are 124 U.S. citizens.

The British liner *Lusitania* was sunk without warning by a German U-boat.

Peninsula – a piece of land surrounded by water on three sides.

KEY WEAPONS: Carrier pigeons

Pigeons could carry messages with up-to-date information many miles from the battlefield. Each side used thousands of pigeons throughout the war. In 1918, for example, the British Army had 20,000 birds managed by a staff of 380 men. Enemy soldiers tried to shoot down pigeons; many birds also died from gas poisoning. Carrier pigeons also took part in naval warfare. Some warships carried birds, for example, as did seaplanes and aircraft on spotting missions over enemy territory.

9 MAY France

General Sir Douglas Haig, commander of the British First Army, attacks on either side of Neuve-Chapelle. The attack grinds to a halt the next day, after 11,600 British casualties. While the British batter away at Aubers Ridge, the French open the Second Battle of Artois.

14 MAY France

The commander of the British Expeditionary Force, Field Marshal Sir John French, is under pressure to support the French offensive in Artois. He sends the First Army to attack Festubert. The British launch their first night attack of the war, but fail to break through the German defences.

19 MAY Turkey

The Australians and New Zealanders at Gallipoli – a total of 17,000 men – defeat an attack by 40,000 Turkish soldiers, inflicting more than 3,000 casualties.

24 MAY Belgium

A German attack at Ypres fails to capture the British-held Bellewaarde Ridge. The fighting ends on 25 May – the last act of the Second Battle of Ypres. British

Australian troops await the order to attack the Turks at Gallipoli.

Seaplane – an aeroplane with floats that can take off from and land on water.

EYEWITNESS: Edith Wharton, U.S. writer, Western Front, 1915

"The church was without aisles, and down the nave stood four rows of wooden cots with brown blankets. In almost every one lay a soldier — the doctor's 'worst cases' — few of them wounded, the greater number stricken with fever, bronchitis, frost-bite, pleurisy, or some other form of trench-sickness too severe to permit them being carried further from the front. One or two heads turned on the pillows as we entered."

losses are 58,000 troops; the Germans have lost 35,000 and the French 10,000.

26 MAY Britain
First Lord of the Admiralty Sir Winston Churchill is fired by Prime Minister Herbert Asquith after the failure of the naval attack on the Dardanelles.

2 JUNE Britain
The government passes the Munitions of War Act to give priority to essential war industries. The act encourages female employment in industry. Some 46,000 women rush to take jobs in British munitions factories.

4 JUNE Turkey
A British attack of some 30,000 men at Gallipoli fails again to capture the Turkish-held town of Krithia.

23 JUNE–7 JULY Italy
The Italians open the First Battle of the Isonzo but make little progress in the moutainous territory. A renewal of the attack on 5 July achieves little. Casualties are heavy: the Italians lose 5,000 men; Austro-Hungarian losses total 10,000.

9 JULY Britain
Secretary of War Lord Kitchener calls for more recruits. By the end of the month, two million men have volunteered for military service.

13 JULY Poland
The German Twelfth Army – 120,000 men – attacks towards Russian-held Warsaw. It has advanced some 8 km (5 miles) by the 17th.

A church in Hull burns after a German airship raid on Britain.

Munitions – ammunition, such as shells for artillery and bullets for guns.

An early British tracked vehicle. It is fitted with a wire cutter at the front.

12 AUGUST Britain

British inventors begin work on what will become the world's first tracked armoured vehicle. Nicknamed 'Little Willie', it makes its debut on 8 September. It is described as a water tank to keep it secret. The term 'tank' enters the common language.

25 SEPTEMBER France

Following a bombardment by 2,500 guns, two French armies attack German trenches, opening the Second Battle of Champagne. The aim is to help Russia by occupying Germany on the western front. The fighting becomes bogged down in November. Another French attack, known as the Third Battle of Artois, also begins. The fighting again continues into November, but the French are unable to break through. British troops commanded by General Sir Douglas Haig also

4 AUGUST Belgium

The Germans arrest British-born nurse Edith Cavell for helping 200 prisoners-of-war to escape. She is convicted by a German court martial on 7 October. Cavell is executed five days later. Her killing turns world opinion against Germany.

TURNING POINTS: Trench warfare

Life in the trenches for the soldiers of both sides was a mixture of boredom and terror. Large-scale battles were rare. Most of the time soldiers in the trenches did guard duty, fetched supplies or repaired or strengthened the trenches. Death was an ever-present danger. The enemy used artillery, machine-gun fire or snipers to inflict casualties. In the winter trenches filled with water, which led to illnesses and diseases. Soldiers had to eat cold food from tins, even in the dead of winter.

Tank – a tracked armoured fighting vehicle.

EYEWITNESS: F. A. McKenzie, British Army, Flanders, 1915

"Rum rations are by now probably served out to all sections of our Flanders troops. They were started in some divisions, I know, in November. Almost every man I have met who has served during the winter is in favour of it. A few convinced teetotallers use it to rub their feet! To most men the drink comes as a glow of light and warmth."

launch an attack, opening the Battle of Loos. The British use gas for the first time in the war. The fighting continues into October.

27–28 SEPTEMBER Mesopotamia
British General Sir Charles Townshend launches his forces against the Turks defending Kut-el-Amara. The Turks suffer 5,300 casualties. British losses are only 1,230.

6 OCTOBER Serbia
Two German and Austro-Hungarian armies invade Serbia from the north. Two Bulgarian armies then invade from the east. Outnumbered by nearly two to one, the Serbian Army is forced to retreat to the southwest.

13–14 OCTOBER France
The British 46th Division captures part of the German-held Hohenzollern Redoubt at the end of the Battle of Loos. British casualties total 62,000 men, while the Germans have about 26,000 men killed, wounded or captured.

23 NOVEMBER Serbia
The Serbian Army – 200,000 men – begins a 160-km (100-mile) retreat, aiming to reach Albania. Short of food and warm clothing, thousands of men die during the withdrawal.

8 DECEMBER Turkey
The evacuation of Allied positions begins at Suvla Bay and Ari Burna at Gallipoli. The Turks do not interfere. Some 83,000 men, 186 artillery pieces, 1,700 vehicles and 4,500 transport animals are taken off the Gallipoli Peninsula.

17 DECEMBER Britain
Field Marshal Sir John French is fired as the commander of the British Expeditionary Force. His replacement is General Sir Douglas Haig.

British troops being evacuated from Gallipoli in December 1915.

Redoubt – a strong, defensive position.

EYEWITNESS: Commandant Raynal, Fort Vaux, Verdun, 1916

"About 8.30 a.m., the Boches carried out two attacks; one against the barricade of the observation post, the other on the barricade of the left arches. Through the loopholes, they poured flame and gas, which gave off an intolerable smell and gripped our throats. Shouts of 'gas masks' came from both ends of the fort. In the left arches, the garrison, driven back by flame and smoke, fell back towards the central gallery."

2 JANUARY, 1916, Black Sea

The British Royal Navy ends a very successful submarine campaign against Turkish shipping. Some 50 percent of Turkey's merchant ships have been sunk.

8 JANUARY Turkey

The Allied evacuation of the Gallipoli Peninsula is completed. The campaign has cost British, Commonwealth and French forces 252,000 casualties, and the Turks some 250,000 men.

1 FEBRUARY English Channel

The British *Franz Fischer* is attacked by Zeppelin airship bombs. It is the first merchant ship to be sunk by air power in warfare.

21 FEBRUARY France

The German offensive against the fortress city of Verdun begins. The main attack is by 140,000 men of Crown Prince William's Fifth Army. The French are pushed back.

22 FEBRUARY France

The French create *La Voie Sacrée* ('The Sacred Way'). This narrow road to Verdun becomes the main route for supplies and reinforcements entering the city. Around Verdun itself, German attacks gain some ground but they are met by fierce French counter-attacks.

25 FEBRUARY France

One of the key French positions at Verdun, Fort Douaumont, falls to German troops. General Henri-Philippe Pétain takes charge of French forces at Verdun. He proclaims *"Ils ne passeront pas"* ("They Shall Not Pass").

French reinforcements rush to Verdun along 'The Sacred Way'.

Merchant ship – a civilian vessel that carries cargo or passengers.

11 MARCH Italy

The Italians begin the Fifth Battle of the Isonzo. The attack against the Austro-Hungarians is in part designed to relieve some of the pressure on the French at Verdun. Little ground is won or lost by either side in the battle.

15 MARCH United States

President Woodrow Wilson orders General John Pershing to invade northern Mexico to track down rebel leader Pancho Villa. Villa's rebels have killed 16 mining engineers, all U.S. citizens, in the United States. Pershing fails to capture Villa.

18 MARCH Russia

The First Battle of Lake Naroch. The Russians launch a major offensive intended to aid the French at Verdun. Some 350,000 Russian soldiers face just 75,000 German troops with

German soldiers guard Russians captured at the Battle of Lake Naroch.

300 field guns. The Russians advance just 1.6 kilometres (1 mile) with the loss of 15,000 men.

14 APRIL Russia

The Russian offensive around Lake Naroch ends. The Russians have lost 122,000 men for little gain. The Germans list 20,000 losses.

TURNING POINTS: Women at war

Women played a greater role than they had in previous wars because the home front was vital. With men away fighting, women were in the majority on the home front. During the war tens of thousands of women worked in factories producing weapons and ammunition (right). By 1918, for example, one-third of German factory workers were women. Women also served as nurses and in uniform behind the front lines, where they drove vehicles. However, female soldiers were a rare sight during the war.

Front line – where the fighting takes place.

The British warship *Queen Mary* blows up at the Battle of Jutland.

31 MAY North Sea

The Battle of Jutland is fought between the British Home Fleet and the German High Seas Fleet. Three British battleships, three cruisers and eight destroyers are sunk for the loss of one German battleship, four cruisers and five destroyers. Although badly damaged, the British fleet is still able to fight on. It makes sure that the High Seas Fleet remains bottled up in its home ports.

21 APRIL Ireland

Irish nationalists rebel against British rule. The rebels take over several of Dublin's public buildings. British troops defeat the uprising on 1 May. More than a dozen captured nationalists will be tried and executed by the British.

29 APRIL Mesopotamia

The besieged British at Kut-el-Amara surrender to the Turks. Of the 13,000 British prisoners, 4,800 will die of sickness or neglect.

13 MAY Arabia

In the first success of their rebellion against the Turks, Arabs fighting for Hussein, Grand Sherif of Mecca, capture the holy city of Mecca.

4 JUNE Russia

Russian forces led by General Aleksey Brusilov launch a major offensive against the Austro-Hungarians and Germans. The Russian attack had been scheduled to coincide with the British attack on the River Somme. Early progress is excellent, particularly in the north and south, where the Austro-Hungarians collapse. In the centre, though, the Germans stand firm.

7 JUNE France

After weeks of bitter fighting, the Germans capture Fort Vaux at Verdun from the French.

17 JUNE Italy

The Austro-Hungarians call a stop to their Trentino Offensive in the face of a mounting

EYEWITNESS: Ernest Francis, HMS *Queen Mary*, Battle of Jutland, 1916

"Flames were belching from what I took to be the fourth ship of the line, then came the big explosion which shook us a bit, and on looking at the pressure gauge I saw the pressure had failed. Immediately after that came what I term the big smash, and I was dangling in the air on a bowline. Everything in the ship went as quiet as a church, the floor of the turret was bulged up and the guns were absolutely useless."

Uprising – a violent rebellion against a government.

Italian counter-attack. The campaign has cost the Italians 147,000 men, including 40,000 taken prisoner. The Austro-Hungarians admit to losses of 81,000, including 26,000 prisoners.

24 JUNE France

The British begin shelling German trenches around the River Somme. Some 2,000 British artillery pieces fire an estimated 1.7 million shells on the first day. However, as many as a third of the shells fail to explode. Many others are too light to inflict much damage on the German barbed wire or their strongly constructed defences.

British troops advancing on the first day of the Battle of the Somme.

1 JULY France

The British Somme Offensive begins. The attacking British infantry are confronted by uncut German barbed wire and intact defences.

Advancing at a walk and burdened down with equipment, the British meet a wall of machine-gun fire. By the end of the day British casualties total more than 57,000, including 19,000 dead. It is the greatest loss ever suffered by the British Army in a single day's combat. German losses are thought to be around 8,000 men.

KEY WEAPONS: Tanks

The tank was developed from farm tractors fitted with caterpillar tracks to prevent wheels from sinking into the ground. The British were the first to develop a tank. 'Big Willie' (right) had a metal box-like body fitted with cannons and machine guns. The crew inside were safe from enemy bullets. However, it was so noisy that crewmen had to communicate by hand signals. The tank's job was to drive across No-Man's Land, crush the enemy's barbed-wire defences and cross their trenches.

Cannon – a large, heavy gun.

EYEWITNESS: Lieutenant Maurice Genevoix, Verdun, 1916

"Not a wink of sleep. The noise of the shells hurtling through the air is constantly in my ears, while the acrid and suffocating fumes of explosives haunt my nostrils. Scarcely yet is it midnight before I receive orders to depart. I emerge from the trusses of wheat and rye among which I had ensconced myself. Bits of stalk have slipped down my collar and up my sleeves, and tickle me all over. The night is so dark."

10 JULY Russia

The Russians have captured 300,000 prisoners since the opening of the Brusilov Offensive.

1 AUGUST France

The British Somme Offensive is a month old. Their casualties total 158,000 plus another 40,000 elsewhere on the Western Front. German losses on the Somme amount to 160,000 men.

4 AUGUST Italy

The Italians launch the Sixth Battle of the Isonzo. They gain some ground, chiefly the town of Gorizia, which falls on 8 August.

Italian troops advance against the Austro-Hungarians at the River Isonzo.

Offensive – a group of military attacks.

KEY WEAPONS: Zeppelin airships

Zeppelins were named after Count Ferdinand von Zeppelin. He produced aluminium-framed airships before the war. They were covered by an outer skin, which contained gas-filled bags that gave lift. By 1914 Germany had a fleet of 18 Zeppelins. Most could reach an altitude of 6,100 metres (20,000 ft) and had a speed of 130 kph (80 mph). Zeppelins dropped 203,000 kg (200 tons) of bombs on Britain in the war, killing 250 people. In return, many Zeppelins were shot down by British and French fighters.

17 AUGUST Italy

The Italians end the Sixth Battle of the Isonzo, their most successful attack so far against the Austro-Hungarians. They have inflicted losses on the enemy of 49,000 for 51,000 Italians.

3 SEPTEMBER Romania

German Field Marshal August von Mackensen, leading a German–Bulgarian–Turkish force known as the Danube Army, invades southern Romania from Bulgaria.

15 SEPTEMBER France

The British begin the Battle of Flers–Courcelette in another attempt to break the deadlock on the Somme. Fourteen divisions are involved in the battle, and tanks appear on the Western Front for the first time. The British manage to capture two villages – Flers and Courcelette – but the slow-moving tanks are far from successful. They cause some panic among the Germans, but many later get knocked out or stuck in mud and ditches, or break down in the advance.

7 OCTOBER United States

Democrat president Woodrow Wilson is re-elected. He has campaigned on a ticket of keeping the United States out of the war.

16 OCTOBER Arabia

The British Captain T.E. Lawrence becomes an adviser to Arab Prince Feisal, who is fighting the Turks. Lawrence will become known as 'Lawrence of Arabia' because of his exploits.

T.E. Lawrence, 'Lawrence of Arabia', photographed in Arab headdress.

Deadlock – a situation in which nothing changes.

TURNING POINTS: Turnip Winter

The winter of 1916–1917 was probably the worst period for German civilians. Heavy rains in late summer were followed by months of very cold weather that wiped out half the potato crop. Potatoes formed a large part of people's food, and by early 1917 many Germans were starving. The turnip had not suffered like the potato, so all kinds of ways were thought up to cook turnips. Turnip Winter was terrible for ordinary Germans. And it made many people angry towards their government (right).

24 OCTOBER France

The French attack northeast of Verdun. They retake Fort Douaumont, with 6,000 prisoners.

18 NOVEMBER France

The Battle of the Ancre marks the end of the British offensive on the Somme. British casualties for the whole offensive are very high – 420,000 men. The French have lost 205,000 troops and the Germans some 500,000. At the end of their attacks, the British have still not captured some of their first-day objectives.

21 NOVEMBER Austria-Hungary

Emperor Franz Joseph dies at the age of 86. He is succeeded by his great nephew, 26-year-old Archduke Charles.

23 NOVEMBER Romania

German Field Marshal August von Mackensen's Danube Army launches a second invasion of Romania. The plan is to link up with the German Ninth Army commanded by General Erich von Falkenhayn, who is advancing through northwest Romania. The two forces make contact on

British troops on shell-blasted land near the River Somme in late 1916.

Mystic – someone who has deeply spiritual beliefs.

EYEWITNESS: Thomas Curtin, U.S. journalist in Berlin, 1916

"The German public has begun to know a great deal about the wounded. They do not yet know all the facts, because wounded men are, as far as possible, hidden in Germany and never sent to centres unless it is absolutely unavoidable. The official figures, which are increasing in an enormous ratio since the development of Britain's war machine, are falsified."

13 DECEMBER Mesopotamia

British General Sir Frederick Maude begins an offensive along the Tigris River. His force of 48,000 men is supported by 24 aircraft and armed river steamers. The Turks have 20,000 troops and 70 artillery pieces. Heavy rains slow the British advance.

15 DECEMBER France

The French attack to the northeast of Verdun. Within a few days, they force the Germans away from key positions, including forts Douaumont and Vaux. This attack ends the main Battle of Verdun. Losses have been enormous for both sides: 360,000 French troops and 336,000 Germans. The German plan to destroy the French Army in 1916 has failed.

31 DECEMBER Russia

Monk and mystic Rasputin, a close friend of the royal family, is murdered by a group of resentful nobles. Many Russians believed he had a bad influence on the royal family, particularly on the czarina (empress).

26 November, by which stage they are less than 80 km (50 miles) from Bucharest, the capital. The defeat of Romania will give the Central Powers access to its oilfields and gas for their vehicles and aeroplanes.

5 DECEMBER Britain

Prime Minister Herbert Asquith resigns as head of the country's coalition government. He is replaced on 7 December by the Liberal leader David Lloyd George. Lloyd George acts swiftly to set up boards and committees to direct the country's war effort.

6 DECEMBER Romania

German Field Marshal August von Mackensen makes a triumphant entry into Bucharest.

A British armed river steamer on the River Tigris shells Turkish positions.

Coalition – an alliance of political parties.

German submarines and destroyers about to sail to attack merchant ships.

an empire in the Pacific, to join the Central Powers. The British intercept and decode this highly sensitive message.

31 JANUARY Germany

The government agrees to launch unrestricted submarine warfare. The Germans know that the United States will declare war if any U.S. vessels are sunk. But they believe they can win victory before the United States can intervene.

3 FEBRUARY United States

The government cuts diplomatic ties with Germany because of the unrestricted submarine warfare campaign.

23 FEBRUARY France

German forces begin a withdrawal to the newly built Hindenburg Line, some 32 km (20 miles) behind the existing front.

19 JANUARY, 1917, Mexico

A German diplomat receives a secret telegram from Foreign Secretary Arthur Zimmermann. Its suggests forming a defensive alliance with Mexico if the United States declares war on Germany. The message also suggests that Mexico should encourage Japan, which wants

TURNING POINTS: Convoys

By 1917, German U-boats were sinking many Allied merchant ships. In response the Allies introduced convoys. The convoy system grouped merchant ships within a protective escort of destroyers and other warships. If German U-boats tried to attack the merchant ships, they risked being attacked themselves by the warship escorts. The system was a success. The first convoy across the Atlantic Ocean sailed in May. Afterwards convoys were introduced for all ocean sailings.

Bolshevik – a left-wing Russian extremist.

30

8 MARCH Russia

Riots, strikes and mass demonstrations break out in Moscow. People are demonstrating against shortages of food and fuel and a government that does not listen to its citizens. The events become known as the 'February Revolution' because the Russian calendar of the time was 11 days behind the Western one.

12 MARCH Russia

Workers and left-wing politicians form the Petrograd Soviet (Council of Workers' Deputies). Two days later the Duma (parliament) itself establishes a government. Neither body accepts the authority of the other. Pressure mounts on the czar to abdicate.

Russia's Czar Nicholas II, who abdicated in the middle of March 1917.

15 MARCH Russia

Czar Nicholas II abdicates.

EYEWITNESS: British nurse Violetta Thurstan, in Russia

"We often saw gangs of prisoners, mostly Austrian, but some German, and they always seemed well treated by the Russians. The Austrian prisoners nearly always looked very miserable, cold, hungry and worn out. Once we saw a spy being put into the train to go to Warsaw, I suppose to be shot – an old Jewish man. How angry the soldiers were with him; one gave him a great punch in the back."

18 MARCH Atlantic Ocean

Three American vessels – *City of Memphis*, *Vigilancia* and *Illinois* – are sunk by German submarines. This incident further angers the United States.

26 MARCH Palestine

British General Sir Archibald Murray begins an invasion of Turkish Palestine with 16,000 troops. The attack fails due to poor planning, water shortages and Turkish resistance. The Turks, who have a similar number of troops in what becomes known as the First Battle of Gaza, suffer 2,500 casualties. The British lose nearly 4,000 men.

3 APRIL Russia

Russian revolutionary Vladimir Ilich Lenin returns from exile to Petrograd. He intends to overthrow the Provisional Government and create a state headed by the Bolsheviks, but must first take control of various soviets (workers' councils). This is achieved by October.

Abdicate – to give up a throne.

An aerial view of the French Nivelle Offensive, which was a total failure.

(4 miles). In the skies overhead, many British aircraft are shot down by German fighters.

11 APRIL France

The British continue the Battle of Arras in the face of growing resistance from the reinforced German Sixth Army under General Ludwig von Falkenhausen. The battle is becoming a stalemate. The British commander-in-chief, Field Marshal Sir Douglas Haig, continues the Arras Offensive into the middle of May. At the end of the offensive British casualties total 150,000 men killed, wounded or captured. German losses are 100,000.

6 APRIL United States

The government of President Woodrow Wilson declares war on Germany.

9 APRIL France

The British begin the Battle of Arras. They aim to force the Germans to withdraw from the River Aisne sector of the Western Front, which is about to be attacked by the French under General Robert Nivelle. The British achieve notable gains on the first day, particularly the Canadian Corps, which captures Vimy Ridge, and its XVII Corps, which advances 6 km

16–20 APRIL France

General Robert Nivelle opens a major French offensive in Champagne and along the River Aisne. Nivelle has 1.2 million men and 7,000 artillery pieces. However, the Germans have captured plans for the attack. French troops are met by artillery and machine-gun fire. Their losses are heavy, some 118,000 men by 20 April.

KEY PEOPLE: Lenin

Vladimir Ilich Lenin (1870–1924) was the leader of the Bolshevik Party. The Bolsheviks emerged as the leading political force in Russia following the 'November Revolution' in 1917. Lenin led the Bolsheviks during the Russian Civil War. After the Civil War Lenin was mainly concerned with extending the Bolsheviks' control of Russia and developing the country's economy. However, he suffered from poor health and had a stroke in 1922. He died in 1924.

Division – a military unit of between 10,000 and 20,000 troops.

Turkish cavalry moves out of a town in Palestine to fight the British.

by taking Samarra on the River Tigris. However, the intense heat forces the British to halt.

9 MAY France

General Robert Nivelle's offensive ends in failure. The French have suffered enormous losses, some 187,000 men as opposed to around 163,000 German casualties.

10 MAY Britain

Prime Minister David Lloyd George orders the British Royal Navy to introduce the convoy system to protect merchant ships from enemy submarines. The system has an immediate impact. German submarine losses rise, while the rate of merchant ship sinkings falls dramatically.

17 APRIL France

A day after the opening of General Robert Nivelle's offensive, the troops of the French 108th Regiment mutiny and abandon their trenches. The mutiny spreads until 68 of the French Army's 112 divisions are involved. Many mutineers are willing to defend their positions, but refuse to attack the enemy.

23 APRIL Mesopotamia

Troops under British General Sir Frederick Maude continue their advance against the Turks

23 MAY Britain

Marking a new chapter in air warfare, 16 long-range German Gotha bombers attack London from their bases in Belgium. Darkness foils the attack on the capital, but the twin-engined aircraft drop their bombs to the east, killing 100 Canadian troops at a military base.

EYEWITNESS: Basil Clarke, observing German prisoners in France

"Marching four abreast along the road came several hundred German prisoners. They carried picks and shovels over their shoulders. They were dressed for the most part in the grey-blue tunics, trousers, little flat caps and the big top-boots of the German Army. Most of them had overcoats too, generally of a dark blue, but into each coat had been sewn a round, circular patch of some bright-coloured cloth, generally red."

Mutiny – a revolt against commanding officers.

EYEWITNESS: Basil Clarke, the Somme, winter of 1917

"In the trenches themselves the difficulty of keeping warm is well-nigh insuperable. For fires are not allowed. It was found that whenever a waft of smoke rose from a trench fire the Germans promptly sent over mortar rounds or shells or hand grenades — feeling pretty sure of course, that wherever there was a fire there also would be a little knot of Tommies gathered round it. And generally, they were right."

7 JUNE Belgium

Field Marshal Sir Douglas Haig's British Expeditionary Force attacks the Messines Ridge in southwest Belgium. The Second Army captures the ridge at a cost of 17,000 casualties. The Germans suffer 25,000 casualties. The British victory paves the way for a big offensive known as the Third Battle of Ypres, or Passchendaele.

1 JULY Russia

Despite growing violence in Russia, the Russian commander-in-chief, General Aleksey Brusilov, launches a major offensive towards Lemberg. It begins well. However, many ordinary Russian soldiers are no longer willing to obey their officers. Many units have established their own soviets (workers' councils) to take decisions. The offensive soon begins to collapse.

24 JULY France

The actress Mata Hari stands trial on charges of spying for the Germans. She is convicted and later executed by the French.

Mata Hari, the German spy (in black hat), about to be shot by the French.

26 JULY France

Faced with growing numbers of enemy warplanes, the Germans form units consisting of around 50 aircraft. One of the most famous, its aircraft painted in bright colours, is named 'Richthofen's Circus' after its commander, Baron Manfred von Richthofen.

31 JULY Belgium

The Third Battle of Ypres, or Passchendaele, begins. Haig aims to smash through the German Fourth Army and then swing north to capture the ports of

'Tommy' – nickname for a British soldier.

An abandoned British tank lies on the muddy battlefield of Passchendaele.

Ostend and Zeebrugge. However, the British advance only 3 km (2 miles).

18 AUGUST–15 SEPTEMBER Italy

The Italian high command launches what becomes the Eleventh Battle of the Isonzo against the Austro-Hungarians. Italian casualties are very high – around 166,000. The Austro-Hungarians have lost 85,000 and are on the point of collapse. They call on their German allies to send forces to stabilize the front.

12 OCTOBER Belgium

The focus of the British offensive at Ypres switches to the village of Passchendaele. This now becomes the main British target.

24 OCTOBER Italy

The Austro-Hungarians, reinforced by several German divisions, open the Twelfth Battle of the Isonzo, also known as the Battle of Caporetto. The opening artillery barrage of explosives and gas causes panic among many front-line Italian units. The troops discover that their masks offer no protection against the enemy gas. By 25 October the Austro-Hungarians have advanced 24 km (15 miles). The Italians order a withdrawal to the River Tagliamento.

KEY WEAPONS: Stormtroopers

German stormtroopers (right) were created to break the trench deadlock on the Western Front. They were trained to get into the enemy's rear areas, creating confusion as they went, rather than fighting against front-line strongpoints. Aircraft and artillery would support the advancing stormtroopers, shooting up enemy targets and pockets of resistance. The stormtroopers were created in 1917. In spring 1918 they came very close to achieving a great German victory on the Western Front.

Strongpoint – a fortified position.

British tanks on their way to lead the attack at the Battle of Cambrai.

French have suffered 85,000 casualties and the Germans list around 260,000 losses.

31 OCTOBER Palestine

British and Commonwealth forces – 88,000 men commanded by General Sir Edmund Allenby – launch the Third Battle of Gaza. Allenby is opposed by some 35,000 Turks commanded by German General Kress von Kressenstein. The battle ends with a daring and successful charge by a brigade of Australian cavalry at dusk. Remarkably, the brigade charges through the Turkish defences and machine-gun fire, taking Beersheba and its vital water wells. The Turks retreat.

26 OCTOBER–10 NOVEMBER Belgium

The British again attempt to capture Passchendaele. The village finally falls on 6 November, ending the offensive that began in late July. In the Third Battle of Ypres the British have suffered 310,000 men killed, wounded or captured to advance just 8 km (5 miles). The

12 NOVEMBER Italy

The Twelfth Battle of the Isonzo, better known as the Battle of Caporetto, ends. It has been a

TURNING POINTS: The Hindenburg Line

The German Hindenburg Line was a defensive position on the Western Front. It actually consisted of three lines. The first line was made up of outposts. They were designed to hold up an enemy attack. The second line was called the 'battle zone'. This line was made up of concrete strongpoints protected by barbed wire (right). The third line was called the 'final line'. This was where the artillery was located. Built in 1917, the Hindenburg Line was a formidable obstacle to any advance.

Outpost – an isolated position occupied by soldiers.

EYEWITNESS: Hamilton Fyfe, British journalist in France, 1917

"Those were the days when the British Army was terribly afraid of war correspondents. It has since learnt that they are like dogs: if they are fed well, and given a warm place to sleep in, and taken out regularly (in motorcars) for exercise and sometimes patted on the head, they behave quite nicely, and give no trouble at all. But, at that early date in the war, they were regarded and treated as desperadoes."

disaster for the Italians. They have suffered around 30,000 men killed or wounded. Some 275,000 prisoners have also been captured by the German and Austro-Hungarian forces. German and Austro-Hungarian casualties total some 20,000 men, a remarkably low figure for such a major offensive.

13–15 NOVEMBER Palestine

British General Sir Edmund Allenby continues his pursuit of the Turkish forces defeated at the Battle of Beersheba. Allenby's troops are able to break through hastily built Turkish defences during the Battle of Junction Station.

20 NOVEMBER France

The Battle of Cambrai, the first big tank battle of the war, takes place. Some 476 British tanks, followed by infantry, attack the German Hindenburg Line. The early attacks are very successful. The Hindenburg Line is pierced to depths of 9–12 km (6–8 miles). The tanks are immune to enemy machine-gun fire. However, many tanks break down, become bogged down in ditches or are smashed by German artillery. The fighting around Cambrai continues into December, with the Germans launching a series of successful counter-attacks.

5 DECEMBER France

The Battle of Cambrai ends. Both the British and German forces have suffered roughly equal casualties – about 40,000 men. The battle has shown that the mass use of tanks can achieve a major breakthrough on the Western Front.

9 DECEMBER Palestine

The Turks abandon the city of Jerusalem. British General Sir Edmund Allenby enters with his forces on 11 December.

British General Sir Edmund Allenby (front) enters the city of Jerusalem.

Brigade – a military unit of around 5,000 troops.

8 JANUARY, 1918, United States

In a speech to Congress, President Woodrow Wilson outlines his 14-Point Peace Plan. It aims to prevent destructive wars by setting up an international body to resolve disputes peacefully.

3 MARCH Russia

The Bolsheviks, who are fighting a civil war in Russia, are forced to sign a harsh peace treaty with the Germans at Brest-Litovsk. The Russians have to give up control of Ukraine, Finland, the Baltic Provinces (Estonia, Latvia and Lithuania), the Caucasus and Poland. They also have to surrender those areas of Russia controlled by 'White' Russians who are opposed to the Bolsheviks.

21 MARCH France

General Erich Ludendorff, the deputy chief of the German General Staff, has planned a knock-out blow on the Western Front before U.S. troops arrive. He aims to attack at the point between the French and British forces in northeast France. The offensive is codenamed Operation Michael. It begins with specially trained stormtrooper units leading the way. The shock of the surprise attack overwhelms the thinly spread British troops.

One of the massive German 'Paris Guns' being test fired.

TURNING POINTS: Wilson's 14 Points

U.S. President Woodrow Wilson (right) devised his 14-Point Peace Programme to prevent the outbreak of future war. At its core was a belief that people had a right to govern themselves. In addition, individual states had a responsibility to join an international body that would solve arguments. It would be called the League of Nations. The League would contain diplomats from all over the world and would settle disputes without waging war.

Codename – the title of a military plan.

EYEWITNESS: Baron Manfred von Richthofen, German air ace, 1918

"I was nearest to the enemy and attacked the man to the rear. To my greatest delight I noticed that he accepted battle and my pleasure was increased when I discovered that his comrades deserted him. So I had once more a single fight. It was a fight similar to the one which I had had in the morning. I fired and he fired without any tangible result. At last I hit him. I noticed a ribbon of white benzine vapour."

23 MARCH Paris
The Germans begin a bombardment of Paris with long-range 21-cm (8-inch) artillery pieces, which become known as the "Paris Guns." The bombardment continues until August 9, killing 256 Parisians and wounding 620.

27 MARCH France
German troops are within striking distance of Amiens, their chief objective. However, the Germans are exhausted and are facing increasing numbers of fresh British and French troops. The German attack is finally halted at the village of Villers-Bretonneux, 16 km (10 miles) to the east of Amiens.

29 MARCH Western Front
U.S. pilot Edward Rickenbacker scores his first air victory. By the end of the war he will be his country's top ace, with 26 kills.

5 APRIL France
General Erich Ludendorff halts Operation Michael. His forces have advanced some 64 km (40 miles) and inflicted around 240,000 casualties on the British and French armies. German losses are equally severe, however.

9–10 APRIL France/Belgium
General Erich Ludendorff opens Operation Georgette against British General Sir Herbert Plumer's Second Army and General Sir Henry Horne's British First Army. Ludendorff uses General Sixt von Arnim's Fourth Army and General Ferdinand von Quast's Sixth Army. The attack begins on the morning of the 9th. The German attack pushes the British back.

U.S. fighter ace Edward Rickenbacker in the cockpit of his fighter aircraft.

Objective – a target to be captured by a military operation.

TURNING POINTS: Air attacks

Air warfare was virtually unknown before World War I. Most generals believed that aircraft had little to contribute. However, by 1918 aircraft were carrying out a wide range of missions. Bombers attacked enemy cities and fighters (right) shot down enemy fighters. Aircraft also provided support for ground troops and collected information on enemy troop movements. In 1914 the French had 141 aircraft. The Germans had 245. By 1918 the French had 3,200 aircraft; the Germans had 2,709.

17 APRIL France/Belgium

British and French troops around Ypres halt the German advance. Both sides have lost around 100,000 troops in the fighting. The German attempt to reach the ports of northern France has failed.

The aftermath of the raid on Zeebrugge, with British ships sunk in the harbour.

21 APRIL Western Front

Baron Manfred von Richthofen, the leading air ace of the war with 80 victories, is shot down and killed during a dogfight.

23 APRIL Belgium

The British launch a surprise assault from the sea to try to stop German submarines and destroyers from Ostend and Zeebrugge operating in the English Channel. At Zeebrugge, *Thetis*, *Intrepid* and *Iphigenia* sail into the inner harbour to block the canal. *Thetis* grounds in the inner harbour. *Intrepid* and *Iphigenia* reach their targets only to be sunk in the wrong position. The attack on Ostend is even less successful.

28 MAY France

U.S. forces undertake their first attack of the war. The fighting centres on the village of Cantigny, to the east of Montdidier. Elements of the U.S. 1st Division under General Robert Lee

Dogfight – a battle between two or more warplanes.

Bullard capture Cantigny, taking 200 prisoners. American losses are 1,600 men.

6 JUNE France

U.S. forces attack at Belleau Wood, to the west of Château-Thierry. After three weeks of fighting the wood is taken. U.S. losses are 1,800 men killed and 7,000 wounded.

15 JUNE Italy

The Austro-Hungarians, now fighting alone against Italy following the withdrawal of German forces to the Western Front, launch what becomes known as the Battle of the Piave River. The offensive is a failure, partly due to the worsening weather and partly also to Italian air attacks. By 22 June the Austro-Hungarians are forced back across the River Piave in disarray. Their casualties total a massive 150,000 men.

15–17 JULY France

German forces begin another major offensive. Their attack along the River Marne is intended to capture ports along the English Channel. The French are aware of the coming offensive thanks to aircraft reconnaissance and to information from German deserters. They launch their own assault. Attacks by the French Ninth Army under General M.A.H. de Mitry halt the German offensive.

EYEWITNESS: William Slavens McNutt, St. Mihiel

"Thousands of American boys were scrambling out of the trenches that had been the painful home of the Allied troops for four slimy, bloody years, and streaming out across that desolate strip of waste that ceased forever to be No-Man's Land as their feet redeemed it, yard by yard, legging it across to the shore of that sea of flame over the German lines."

16–17 JULY Russia

Several members of the Russian royal family, including Czar Nicholas II, the Czarina and their children, are murdered by Bolsheviks at Ekaterinburg, Siberia.

18 JULY France

French, British and U.S. forces launch a counter-attack against German forces in Champagne. The fighting becomes known as the Second Battle of the Marne. The main attack involves the French Tenth Army and is spearheaded by the U.S. 1st and 2nd Divisions. The German defenders begin to collapse under these attacks.

U.S. troops advance during the Battle of Cantigny at the end of May.

Deserter – a soldier who abandons his position without permission.

U.S. troops with French tanks in the Meuse-Argonne area of the front.

8 AUGUST France

Field Marshal Sir Douglas Haig's British Expeditionary Force leads what becomes known as the Amiens Offensive. More than 400 tanks lead the advance. Some German front-line units simply flee the fighting. About 15,000 men surrender. When news reaches General Erich Ludendorff, he calls 8 August the 'Black Day of the German Army'. By 12 August the Germans have lost 40,000 men killed or wounded and 33,000 taken prisoner. British and French losses total 46,000 troops.

6 AUGUST France

The Second Battle of the Marne ends. It has been a disaster for the German forces, who have lost 168,000 men. Casualties are huge among their best-trained troops – the stormtrooper units. The stormtroopers who have survived are now suffering from very low morale.

12–16 SEPTEMBER France

The American Expeditionary Corps and the French II Colonial Corps launch an attack on the salient at St. Mihiel, south of Verdun. It has been held by the Germans since 1914. The attack begins in thick fog but is supported by

TURNING POINTS: African Americans

Some 2,291,000 African Americans volunteered for service, and another 367,000 were drafted. The U.S. Marines and Army Air Force Service refused to take black volunteers, however. In the U.S. Army and Navy many black volunteers were given menial jobs. When given the chance, however, African Americans excelled in battle. The 369th Regiment (right) was nicknamed the 'Harlem Hellfighters'. It so impressed the French that they awarded it the *Croix de Guerre* for high valour.

Morale – the emotional and spiritual strength of soldiers.

●●●●●● ● ● ● ● ●●●●●●●●●●●●● ● ●●●●●●

EYEWITNESS: Unknown American soldier, France, 1918

"We passed by riddled German sign-boards, and came to a litter of wreckage that had once been a village, and then we left the main road and entered a little wood — an assembly of scarred tree trunks leaning at all angles. It was crossed by a zigzag trench and all the refuse of battle lay scattered about. We marched in silence through this dismal land of ruin."

600 aircraft. German resistance collapses on the first day. The U.S. troops capture 15,000 German prisoners and 250 guns at a cost of 7,000 casualties.

19–21 SEPTEMBER Palestine

British General Sir Edmund Allenby opens what becomes known as the Battle of Megiddo against 44,000 Turks. The Turks are demoralized and short of supplies. The British offensive begins at 04:30 hours with an artillery bombardment. The British then attack along the Mediterranean coast. The Turks are defeated and some 25,000 prisoners are captured.

26 SEPTEMBER–3 OCTOBER France

The U.S. First Army – around one million men – launches the Meuse–Argonne Offensive to the north of Verdun. U.S. forces make rapid gains, advancing about 16 km (10 miles) in the first five days of the offensive.

27 SEPTEMBER France

Parts of the British Expeditionary Force and French units attack towards Cambrai and St. Quentin to break through the German Hindenburg Line. Allied units are at first slowed by the waterlogged terrain. However,

they force the Germans to abandon the Hindenburg Line altogether on 4 October.

1 OCTOBER Syria

British forces enter Damascus, taking 20,000 Turkish prisoners as they do so.

17–31 OCTOBER France

British forces punch through the German defenders holding the line of the Selle River, taking 20,000 prisoners.

Some of the thousands of Germans taken prisoner by the British in October.

Draft – to make citizens become members of the armed forces.

TURNING POINTS: Casualties

When the conflict ended, the scale of destruction and the loss of life was unparalleled in human history. From August 1914 until November 1918, rarely a day went by when there was no military activity. Out of the 65 million troops mobilized by all of the fighting nations, some eight million were killed and a further 21 million wounded.
The loss of life in combat was mirrored in civilian casualties that were also unparalleled. Some 6.6 million civilians died, chiefly in Russia and Turkey.

23 OCTOBER Italy

The Battle of Vittorio Veneto. The Italians attack Austro-Hungarian forces in northern Italy. Initially, the battle goes well for the Austro-Hungarians, who block the advance of the Italian Eighth Army as it tries to cross the River Piave. However, the Italian Twelfth Army, commanded by French General Jean Graziani, gains a foothold on the Austro-Hungarian side of the Piave.

29 OCTOBER Germany

Sailors of the German High Seas Fleet mutiny at the naval base at Kiel. They are protesting the decision of their new commander, Admiral Franz von Hipper, to make a last 'death ride' against the British Home Fleet. Uprisings break out across Germany. The government decides to make peace before there is a revolution.

30 OCTOBER Italy

In the ongoing Battle of Vittorio Veneto, it is clear that the Austro-Hungarian forces are disintegrating. The fighting officially ends on 3 November. The Austro-Hungarians have lost some 300,000 troops taken prisoner, while Italian casualties total just 38,000 men.

1 NOVEMBER France

The final stage of the U.S.-led Meuse–Argonne Offensive begins. German resistance is falling apart. U.S. forces move rapidly along the valley of the River Meuse in the direction of Sedan,

Germany's Kaiser Wilhelm II (third from right) leaves Germany to go into exile.

Armistice – a halt in the fighting agreed by both sides.

EYEWITNESS: Edward Wright, British Army, November 1918

"Behind the British soldiers in the liberated towns of Belgium was a whirl of dancing joy. Soldiers and girls, staid matrons and stiff officers, swayed hand-in-hand down the streets, singing in an ecstasy of happiness, or playing kiss-in-the-ring. There were more solemn scenes of joy in the cities of Lorraine and Alsace while the Americans and French were preparing to cross the hostile frontier."

which falls on 6 November. Germany has no option but to request an armistice.

3 NOVEMBER Austria-Hungary

Following their catastrophic defeat at Vittorio Veneto, the Austro-Hungarians seek an armistice with Italy. It is agreed the next day.

9 NOVEMBER Germany

Kaiser Wilhelm II abdicates the German throne. He goes into exile in the Netherlands the next day. A new chancellor, Friedrich Ebert, and a new government are appointed the next day. However, Germany is politically unstable. Various left- and right-wing political groups are struggling for control.

11 NOVEMBER Europe

The armistice on the Western Front, negotiated over four days at Compiègne, comes into force at 11:00 hours. World War I is over.

14 NOVEMBER Czechoslovakia

Czechoslovakia, part of the Austro-Hungarian Empire, becomes an independent republic.

17 NOVEMBER Germany

Under the terms of the armistice, German forces begin to leave those parts of France and Belgium that they still occupy.

1 DECEMBER Germany

British, French and U.S. forces move into the Rhineland as part of the armistice terms.

13 DECEMBER France

Woodrow Wilson arrives in France – the first president to travel outside the United States.

People in Paris, France, celebrate the end of World War I in November 1918.

Republic – a country ruled by a president.

45

Glossary

abdicate: to give up a throne

armistice: a halt in the fighting agreed by both sides

blockade: the closing off of a country's trade using warships

Bolshevik: a left-wing Russian extremist

bombard: to attack with artillery

brigade: a military unit of around 5,000 troops

cannon: a large, heavy gun

coalition: an alliance of political parties

codename: the title of a military plan

counter-attack: an attack by a defending force

cruiser: a fast, heavily armed warship

deadlock a situation in which nothing changes

deserter: a soldier who abandons his position without permission

division: a military unit of between 10,000 and 20,000 troops

dogfight: a battle between two or more warplanes

draft: to make citizens become members of the armed forces

expeditionary force: part of an army sent to fight in a foreign country

flank: the right or left wing of an army

front line: where the fighting takes place

howitzer: a type of field gun

merchant ship: a civilian vessel that carries cargo or passengers

morale: the emotional and spiritual strength of soldiers

munitions: ammunition, such as shells for artillery and bullets for guns

mutiny: a revolt against commanding officers

mystic: someone who has deeply spiritual beliefs

neutral: not taking sides in a dispute or war

objective: a target to be captured by a military operation

offensive: a group of military attacks

outpost: an isolated position occupied by soldiers

peninsula: a piece of land surrounded by water on three sides

propaganda: material that spreads ideas or rumours to help one side in a war

redoubt: a strong defensive position

republic: a country ruled by a president

salient: a part of a front line that projects into enemy territory

seaplane: an airplane with floats that can take off from land and water

strongpoint: a fortified position

tank: a tracked armoured fighting vehicle

Tommy: nickname for a British soldier

uprising: a violent rebellion against a government

Zeppelin: a long, thin, motor-powered airship

Further resources

BOOKS ABOUT WORLD WAR I

World War I (DK Eyewitness Books), DK Children, 2007

Key Battles of World War I (20th Century Perspectives) by David Taylor, Heinemann, 2001

My First World War (My War) by Daniel James, Franklin Watts, 2008

Going to War in World War One (A Soldier's Life) by Fiona Corbridge, Franklin Watts, 2006

The First World War by Dennis Hamley, Franklin Watts, 2005

World War I (Timelines) by Stewart Ross, Franklin Watts, 2007

The First World War (How Did It Happen?) by Reg Grant, Franklin Watts, 2007

USEFUL WEBSITES

www.firstworldwar.com

www.bbc.co.uk/history/worldwars/wwone

www.spartacus.schoolnet.co.uk/FWW.htm

www.worldwar1.com

www.pbs.org/greatwar

www.eyewitnesstohistory.com/w1frm.htm

Index